C000145159

Contents

1812 Overture

Peter Ilyich Tchaikovsky
Arranged by Carol Matz

Moderately fast

EASY PIANO 1150

Simply Romantic Era

24 Well Known Masterpieces

Arranged by Carol Matz

Simply Romantic Era is a collection of arias, choral works, piano masterpieces, symphonic themes, and other famous works from the Romantic period of music history (ca. 1820–1910). These selections have been carefully arranged by Carol Matz for Easy Piano, making them accessible to pianists of all ages. Phrase markings, fingering, pedaling and dynamics have been included to aid with interpretation, and a large print size makes the notation easy to read.

The Romantic era includes a diverse and exciting body of music. Some of the world's most beloved melodies come from this era, and continue to be as relevant today as the day they were composed. Tchaikovsky's rousing *1812 Overture*—and its signature cannon blasts—has become a staple of Independence Day celebrations in the United States. Gounod's *Funeral March of a Marionette* is inexorably linked with the classic television show *Alfred Hitchcock Presents*. During the Romantic era, opera came to the forefront as composers created massive spectacles while plumbing the depths of human emotion. From the plaintive longing of Puccini's *Un bel dì*, to the comic bitterness of Verdi's *La donna è mobile*, to the ecstatic joy of Offenbach's *Can-Can*, opera takes audiences on a unique journey. The Romantic era also saw the modernization of the piano, and composers responded by expanding the expressiveness and technical breadth of the instrument. Chopin's endless gift for melody is evident in his *Nocturnes*, as is Brahms's mastery of structure in his *Waltzes*. With its soaring highs and heart-wrenching lows, and its ability to tell richly realized stories, music from the Romantic era has been embraced by musicians and audiences, young and old, around the world. For these reasons and more, the selections on the following pages are exciting to explore.

After all, this is *Simply Romantic Era!*

ISBN-10: 0-7390-5180-6
ISBN-13: 978-0-7390-5180-1

9
mf
f
12
15
mf
18

21
24
27
30

Andaluza

(No. 5 from *12 Spanish Dances*)

Enrique Granados
Arranged by Carol Matz

13
16
mf
19
22
mp

25
poco rit.
28
a tempo
31
molto rit.
34
a tempo
rit.
pp
8va

Anitra's Dance

(from *Peer Gynt Suite*)

Edvard Grieg
Arranged by Carol Matz

13
16
f
19
ff
8va
Fine
mf
22

25
p
29
mf
33
p
mp
37

41
45
49
mf
53
D. S. al Fine
molto rit.
p

Barcarolle

(from *The Tales of Hoffmann*)

Jacques Offenbach
Arranged by Carol Matz

9
12
15
18
mf

21
24
27
a tempo
poco rit.
mp
30
simile

33
36
mf
39
42
mp
p

Bridal Chorus

(from *Lohengrin*)

Richard Wagner
Arranged by Carol Matz

11
15
mp
19
f
mp
23
mf
f

27
31
35
39
poco rit.
mp

Can-Can

(from *Orpheus in the Underworld*)

Jacques Offenbach
Arranged by Carol Matz

13
17
f
p
21
f
mp
25
f

29
32
35
39
ff
8va

Funeral March of a Marionette

Charles Gounod
Arranged by Carol Matz

9
p
12
mf
15
f
p
18
f
p

21
f
mf
24
p
27
mf
30
f

Habanera

(from *Carmen*)

Georges Bizet

Arranged by Carol Matz

9
12
15
mf
18

21
24
f
mp
27
a tempo
poco rit.
f
mf
30
a tempo
molto rit.
f
8va

In the Hall of the Mountain King

(from *Peer Gynt Suite*)

Edvard Grieg
Arranged by Carol Matz

10
mp
13
16
19
mf

22
8va
f
25
29
8va
f
ff
ff
33
p
ff
sfz

"Italian" Symphony

(First Movement Theme)

Felix Mendelssohn
Arranged by Carol Matz

9
12
15
18
f

21
mp
24
27
f
30
ff

La donna è mobile

(from *Rigoletto*)

Giuseppe Verdi

Arranged by Carol Matz

10
13
16
mp
19
cresc.
f
rit.

22
a tempo
mf
25
p
mf
29
32
f
ff

Morning Mood

(from *Peer Gynt Suite*)

Edvard Grieg
Arranged by Carol Matz

17
21
25
29

33
f
37
mf
mp
41
p
45
pp

Merry Widow Waltz

(from *The Merry Widow*)

Franz Lehár
Arranged by Carol Matz

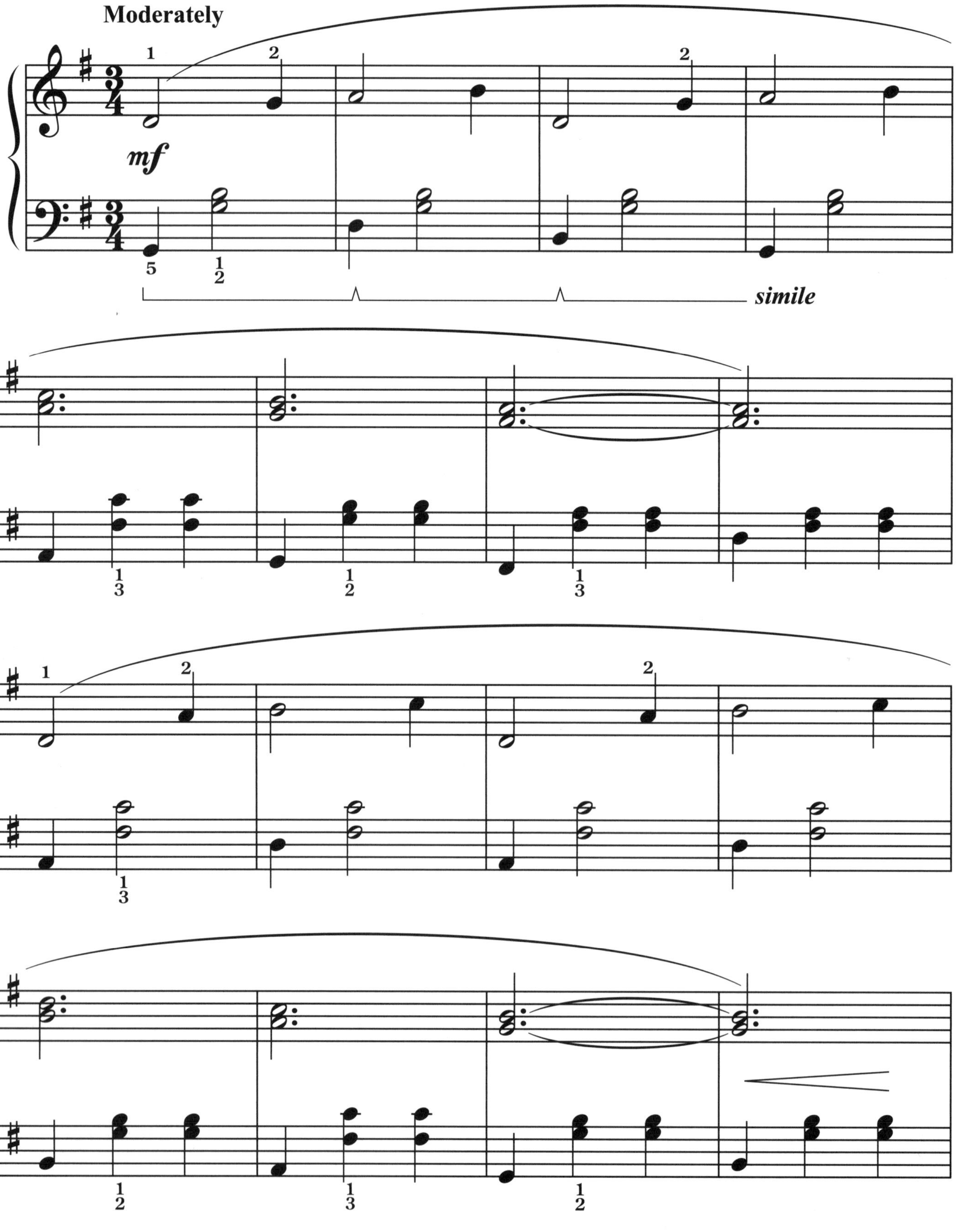

17
f
21
25
mp
29
p

Nocturne

(Op. 55, No. 1)

Frédéric Chopin
Arranged by Carol Matz

2.
9
12
mf
14
p
17
rit.
a tempo

20
22
mf
25
p
28
mf

30
p
33
a tempo
rit.
36
mf
39
mp
p rit.

"New World" Symphony

(Second Movement Theme)

Antonín Dvořák
Arranged by Carol Matz

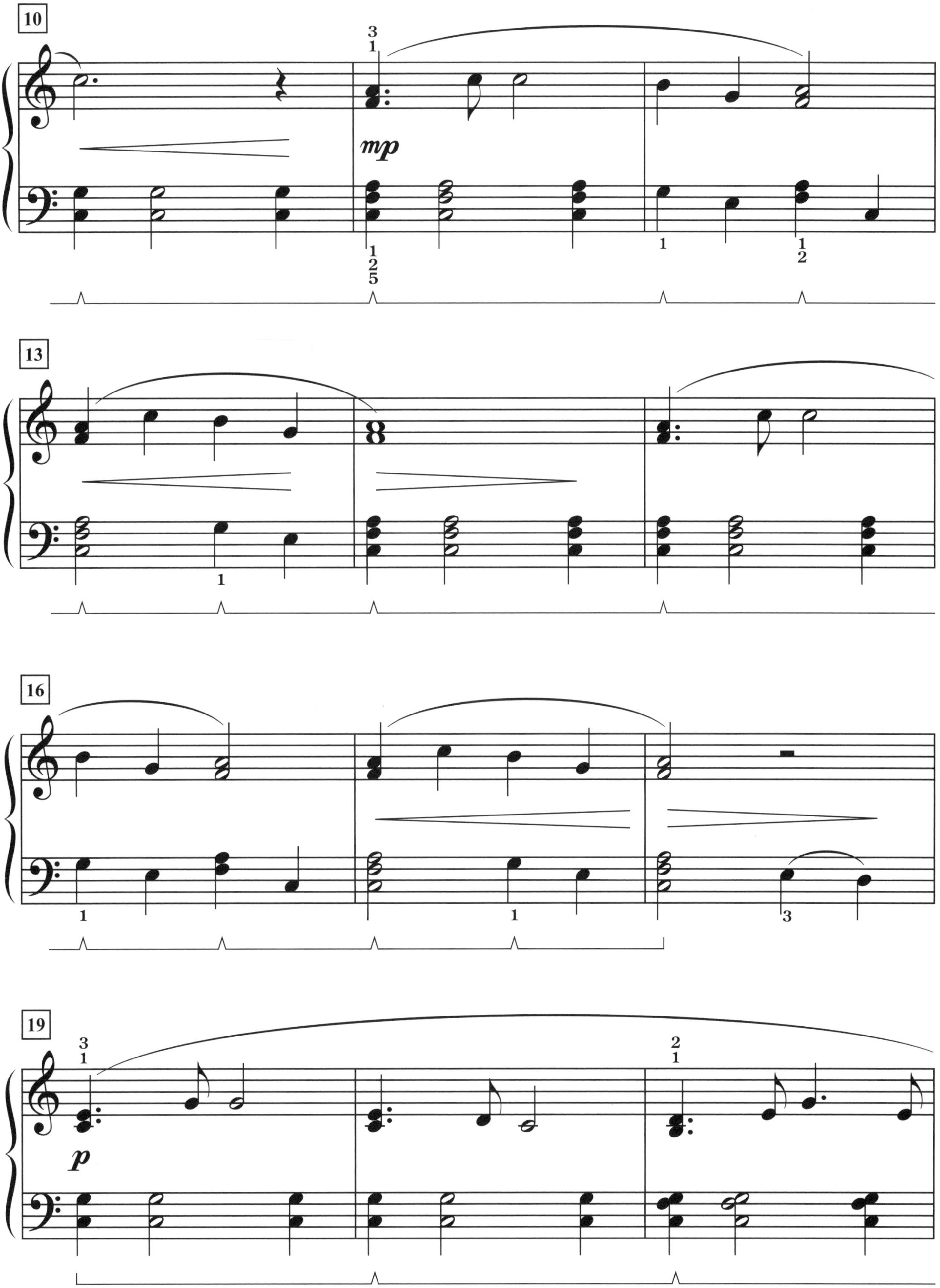
10
mp
13
16
19
p

22
25
f
27
mp
Slower
p
30
LH
rit.
pp
8va

Piano Concerto No. 1

(First Movement Theme)

Peter Ilyich Tchaikovsky
Arranged by Carol Matz

11
14
17
20

23
mp
simile
26
29
32
p rit.
pp

O mio babbino caro

(from *Gianni Schicchi*)

Giacomo Puccini
Arranged by Carol Matz

9
12
15
mp
18

21
24
mf
27
mp
30
f

33
36
mp
39
42
LH over
rit.
p

Polovetsian Dance
(from *Prince Igor*)

Alexander Borodin
Arranged by Carol Matz

9
mf
12
15
mp
18

21
mf
24
mp
27
p
30
rit.
pp

Ständchen
(Serenade)

Franz Schubert
Arranged by Carol Matz

11
mp
14
p
17
mf
20
p

23
mf
26
f
29
mp
32
p
poco rit.
pp

The Swan

(from *Carnival of the Animals*)

Camille Saint-Saëns
Arranged by Carol Matz

13
mp
16
19
mf
22

25
p
29
mp
33
rit.
37
a tempo
mp

41
45
mp
49
p
molto rit.
a tempo
8va
53
RH
LH
LH over
rit.
pp

Swan Lake

(Act I, Finale Theme)

Peter Ilyich Tchaikovsky
Arranged by Carol Matz

Flowing

17
mf
simile
21
mp
26
mf
31
f
rit.

35
a tempo
mp
39
43
47
p
molto rit.
pp
8va

Un bel dì

(from *Madame Butterfly*)

Giacomo Puccini
Arranged by Carol Matz

11
mf
14
17
mp
20

24
mf
rit.
27
Tempo I
f
30
mp
p
33
rit.
pp

Vocalise

Sergei Rachmaninoff
Arranged by Carol Matz

10
mf
13
16
f
19

22
mp
f
25
mf
28
p
31
pp

34
a tempo
rit.
p
37
40
43
rit.
pp

Waltz

(Op. 39, No. 15)

Johannes Brahms

Arranged by Carol Matz